Whispers
of a
Soul

C. Tarantino

First Edition

ISBN: 979-8-9905714-0-2

Cover Design: Cuadrado

readlotsofpages@gmail.com

Disclaimer

DEDICATION

To the oppressed, whose voices echo through silence,
and to all who seek light in the darkest of nights.

ACKNOWLEDGMENTS

Alhamdulillah, all praise and thanks belong to Allah, without Whose mercy and guidance these words would not exist.

I am deeply grateful to my family for their patience, love, and unwavering support.

I am also extending a heartfelt thank you to the communities standing firm against oppression, whose resilience and courage inspired many of these pages. And to the readers: you are the reason these words come alive. May they remind us of our purpose, awaken our hearts, and bring us closer to the eternal home of Jannah.

CONTENTS

FRIENDS

A prick of a thorn
An expiation for your sin
How many have you committed today
Are you that eager to let Shaitan win

Some say it's easy to restrain
Some say it's hard
You go through the day uncaring
You are becoming scared

Scared by your thoughts
Which then turn into actions
Your surrounding is your downfall
With the many attractions

Free yourself of your friends too
Who will lead you astray
Not towards Allah and His Messenger
But the opposite, far far away

ISLAM

Allah guides whom He will
No need for a torch on the foothills

Your path will be shown to you
No need to wait in a queue

Unless you see your life as such
With all the hardships and the crutch

Preparing you for precisely this time
So that you can undertake this climb

WITH EASE

Against the wind I am shouting
Amid thundering and lightning
The vast meadow I am scouting
Fear – my companion – I am fighting

Be brave and strong I whisper
Walking through this darkness alone
Behind I left my sisters
I am brave and strong – and grown

My bravery extends to my shout
Full of longing climbing through the trees
The path I take without a doubt
Is given by Allah with ease

RIGHT PATH

Like dandelions pollen in the air
Settling in the east and west
My life's odyssey – a huge quest
Filled with dare and despair

    Such is life – being pulled by a rope
    Being molded and shaped in a way
    Never fall in despair – always have hope
    With patience and growth you will not stray

        You will not stray from the path
        That was pre-destined for you
        Helping you to avoid Allah's wrath
        Which would bring you to Hell's queue

BLESSED

A millionaire but not in numbers – I am blessed
With as much pollen as a dandelion in the west
With as many life journeys in my chest

I am on this earth just a guest
Treading lightly on my conquest
With contentment and gratitude – I rest

On the shores of the oceans in the west
Or the eastern mountain breast
I sit here and enjoy the golden crest

Like I said before – I am blessed
Enjoying life as I can to the fullest
But only within Allah's boundaries – I attest

STILL ALIVE

Why do you weep
Over your life
You are not yet asleep

Rather you need to strive
Hold your head high
Because you are still alive

Not a sob or a sigh
Is permitted for thee
And you might ask why

Because of the blessings' I see
Too many to count
I am sure you might agree

So go on and dismount
To increase your blessings amount

LACKING

My scars are medals
for my life's despair
honing them like a warrior
only with no pride and care

How could I be prideful
of such a careless life
with deeds deemed frightful
lacking honor and strive

GUIDED

Am I dreaming
My eyes open wide
The night suddenly bright
Reality takes over

My perception of things
Changing over time
Leaving me to my prime
Life just became sweeter

Sweeter – like the sunrise glow
Grazing the horizon line
Or the mountains catching its shine
What a splendid view from here

Awoken from a slumber
In the deepest of the night
Guided by my Lord to the light
Oh, what an immeasurable blessing

I am dreaming no more
Wondering with purpose now
To one alone I now bow
A life filled with gratitude

FAJR

It is quiet on this morning day
The thick fog turning it all gray
Will I hear the sounds of birds?

The world, still sleeping while I pray
Standing here – but I am far away
Chirping sounds, I thought I heard

A little longer - I wish they would stay
Singing on this chilly morning in May
Praying to their Lord with their own words

PREPARE

Life goes by in the blink of an eye
If they told you different – it's a lie
Prepare before you have to say goodbye

Prepare not with money and fame
Like the ones before you who came
You could not put upon them your blame

Prepare yourself with prayer and good deeds
That are like sowing in the ground good seeds
That will overtake the bad weeds

MY PEOPLE

I was born and raised in Germany
At birth already a foreigner
My parents from a country around the corner
Where did I belong?

It must have been my passport
From a different country – Spain
Where the language was other than plain
Where my parents still felt they belonged

Germany was my country now
If only by name
And without any claim
Fluent though yet not accepted

Spain how beautiful you were
Four weeks of yearly vacation fun
Pretending I belonged to you as one
Until you called me the "German Girl"

In one a foreigner, in the other a German
But in two cultures immersed

For acceptance I thirst
Am I to be without people?

Then I accepted Islam and realized
That I was a foreigner no more
I was the opposite of poor
I had found my people

GONE FLAME

The shame is real
The disappointment hard as steel
Through the world I reel

Unsteady as a fawn
My pride vanished – all gone
My head held low far beyond dawn

The lingering haze of shame
My treasure a gone flame
I have only myself to blame

How can I be rectified
From my shame to be untied
With my head held high in stride

My deeds can pose no more danger
These are the pleas of a changer
Thus, I have to become a stranger

FATE

A new year has supposedly started
Today is the first day
Where last year's gray clouds have parted
I now see the sun's ray

Everything seems better now
My thoughts can hardly be contained
I have all answers to my questions – how
And I am not even drained

But why is today's sun shining
And yesterday it was still gray
Maybe it's the rose color glasses lining
My face that fell to your lies prey

The lies that followed me all year long
Telling me that next year will be great
My troubles and fears will be long gone
Changed will be my fate

In truth no changes have occurred
The sun is just now out
I am regretful that I have been lured
To a year full of doubt

My fate no matter what year
Is determined by Allah alone
I need no new year cheer
To feel that I have grown

EARTHQUAKE

The earth shook
In the tranquil of the night
Families tucked in
Where they couldn't see the light

Bright as it was shining
Contrast to the black sky
Unbeknownst to the world
That this night martyrs will die

Devastation and chaos
People calling out
The only one who can help
Is Allah – without a doubt

Ya Allah, help the people
Free them from the rubble
Shed your mercy on them
And take all of their trouble
Amin

SWEET RIVER

The rivers of honey and milk
Flowing in abundance so sweet
No worries and no fears
Left behind would be the white sheet

One trial in this Dunya
Another in the grave
Uncertainty overwhelms me – I want
From the hell fire to be safe

No amount of deeds will suffice
Compared to all the blessings bestowed
Allah's mercy is the only way to Jannah
There's my eternal abode

TIME WASTED

The minutes are passing by
Like the river in motion
Billions of droplets adding – becoming one
Eventually flowing into the ocean

Time keeps on ticking by
Like the dripping sound outside
Gaining speed over time
Until the rain stops and you have died

Regret will fill your heart
You are utterly unprepared
The river of time you have wasted
Now you are in the grave alone and scared

BIRDS SONG

I opened my eyes
To this dreary day
With gray mist in the skies

Thunder and lightning were also at play
Worshipping the most high
As we may

I must not tell a lie
There is nothing dreary here
Only beauty that I spy

The firmament might not be clear
The rainbow in the afternoon
Only unspeakable beauty here

Can you hear the tune
The beautiful birds' tune

RAMADAN

No sustenance for the day
The wrong explanations made
To feel like the poor, they say
This is incorrect, I am afraid

Ramadan is to worship our Lord
The most high – above his throne
The rewards are still to be explored
Until then it belongs to the unknown

But know this
The reward is unmeasurable
In Jannah with eternal bliss
Compared to this life, preferable

So no, we don't fast to feel like the poor
Surely it is an emotional aftereffect infliction
But we want to enter through Jannah's door
And not have a hell fire eviction

NECTAR

A drop of my tea
The sweet honey
Provided by the bee

Whose humming fills the air
The sweetness of nectar
And the silent prayer

From flower to flower
The destined path and even further
Until the final hour

This will be a time
When we're all brought
To be judged for our crimes

So be good to the bee
Whom Allah sent to provide you
With sweet honey for your tea

TRAVELER

Be like the traveler here
  Leaving moist footsteps
    Wondering the sphere

A traveler knows its aim
  Avoiding lewdness – indecency
    And its encompassing shame

So be like the morning dew
  A mirage of beauty, brace yourself
    The better place awaits you

TURNING FREE

Am I too late?
Have I sealed my fate?
Arrogantly going through life without fear
Is this how I got here?

Thinking it was all just a game
Competing for this dunya's fame
Lewdness and indecency I didn't mind
How could I have been so blind

Till my last breath I have time
To turn around and repent for my crimes
I will start tomorrow
I say to myself with sorrow

For the truth that lies within me
And the fear of not becoming free
I will start tomorrow I say again
Having my heart cleansed by the blessed rain

Pouring over me like a loving friend
I want a good end
I want a good end

QADR

This is exactly
Where I'm supposed to be
Free, like drifting in the open sea

Like floating above the clouds
Where only angels stay
There, to Allah they pray

Why did I think
I should be elsewhere
When Allah is the planner of all my affairs

This is why I am at peace
Drifting in life's open sea
Knowing, this is where I am supposed to be

HOT COALS

Bravery is being hated
Fear is being exaggerated
Society is heading towards a slope
Make sure to hold tight to the rope

Don't be deceived by today's liars
Who are the fuel for the fires
It is a trying time on earth for souls
Like holding on to hot coals

So fill your life with peace and calm
And hold on tight to your Islam
Do not waver from the straight path
So you can be safe from Allah's wrath

THE GLOW

There used to be a time
I felt very alone
It felt like an endless climb
To a future unknown

What was I missing in my life
That made me feel so
Was it the money and the worldly strife
Or was it the spiritual glow

The glow emitting from a person's face
When their lifestyle is Islam
Constantly worshipping to erase
Their sins – replacing it with calm

The calm that is lacking in my life
With loneliness suffocating me
The need for change and strive
The need for spirituality

I know what I must do now
To adopt the way of life – Islam
So I can ask daily when I bow
For the glow and the calm

BOW DOWN

Imagine you could not smell
The air before a sunset
Fresh flowers on the meadow
Or the rain that hasn't come yet

Imagine you could not hear
The waves of the ocean
The seagull's calling out
Or your loved ones devotion

Imagine you could not see
The sun on the horizon line
The changing of the leaves
Or the ripe grapes on the vine

Imagine you could do
All those things and more
So, be grateful to Allah
And put your head on the floor

JANNAH

I always thought I was happy
Before I accepted Islam
And how could one measure happiness
Without ever feeling the calm

The calm that comes with the knowledge
That we have a purpose here in life
To worship only one – Allah
And for His mercy to constantly strive

We are encouraged to be good to animals
And for people never to harm one another
To give everyone their rights
Especially to our mothers

We know that even a smile
Counts on our scales as a good deed
Though no deeds will be enough to enter Jannah
We need Allah's mercy to succeed

So, I know, this life is only temporary
My home in Paradise already built for me
It's up to choose it with my actions here
To live in Paradise in peace for eternity

SIGNS

The major signs are quickly coming to pass
The water through cities is raging
Trees are being pulled out of the grass
And the earth is frequently shaking

Are you awake yet
To start to pray five times a day
Pay off all your debts
And from sins stay far away

Judgment day will not wait for you
The horn will signal the start
To our intercessors we will look to
And in fear we will all take part

CAGELESS

With every line
I draw on an empty page
I am drawing my life
But without the cage

You see
I am free of all social expectation
I'm in no need to flaunt my beauty
Because I know my worth – my Station

FIGHT EVIL

everyone believes that snow is cold
and everything it touches dies
they believe it's merciless and empty
like some people's hearts and eyes

but nothing can be compared
to the frigid hearts in their chests
they can hardly be called people
they are evil pests

for their own gain and power
they would go to any length
so we fight their vicious plans
united – with all our strength

MY CHARACTER

It is an everyday struggle
To keep this Dunya out
To keep my heart clean
And without any of the doubts

It is an everyday struggle
To say only what's good
To give the benefit of the doubt
And make excuses like I should

It is an everyday struggle
To be kind to everyone
Even to the aggressor
That of my religion makes fun

But I know the worth of these struggles
Who seems at times to overcome me
I am not of perfect character
But I try my hardest to be

MY MIND

I   walked through   the   fog
Once   again today
Disoriented   as   usual
Until I started to pray

With every step thereafter
I could see in front of me
The Clarity in Life
That before I couldn't see

So, I kept on praying
Until the fog cleared
Then I looked inside
And saw nothing that I feared

PALESTINE

PALESTINE

Your silence will be your enemy
On the days of days
Complacent to the crime
Almost like brothers in the blaze

The lives that have been taken
Not just now, but have been for years
Supported by the ignorant
Who shed for the oppressors' tears

Your crocodile tears are as wasted
As your deeds on this earth
Your compassion driven by money
You will find out soon enough its worth

FLOWERS IN MEADOWS

I want to write about beautiful flowers
Growing on vast meadows
But what comes to mind are children's tears
And their lifeless bodies in the shadows

Their dreams and ambitions
Are now a thing of the past
A life short lived
"Why was I killed?" they will ask

War, a concept not foreign
But a part of everyday life
The flowers in the meadow
Awaiting them in the afterlife

GAZA

I feel like I am dreaming
But not just any dream
The window through which I'm gleaming
Portrays the horrors I now see

Depicted only as numbers
Or worse animals alike
Being killed by the thousand
No mercy when they strike

While the children cry in pain
The parents cry in despair
The aggressor does not abstain
From dropping more bombs

I feel like I am dreaming
Because there is nothing I can do
I cannot close the window
To the genocide in view

MARTYR

They are not among us anymore
Have been taken from this world
Labeled a martyr in this war
And what a beautiful honor it is

Only the martyrs will want to return
To get a second chance
To die in Allah's path again
And against falsehood to take a stance.

Do not say they are dead
Because they surely are alive
They are enjoying Paradise instead
Reunited with their loved ones

They gained the ultimate victory
By being patient here
Now they have all eternity
To Allah and the Prophet to be near

YOUR TIME WILL COME

It all started on October seventh
When you were allegedly attacked
From an army you deem as terrorists
But are those really the facts?

The date was actually 1948
When you took over their land
You didn't call yourself terrorists
Your plan was to expand

Back then Palestinians took you in
You were illegal immigrants in need
So, you repaid them with theft and despair
Your occupation led by evil greed

No this land is not your birthright
You stole it by force
By killing and plundering innocent people
With not an ounce of remorse

But make no mistake
Your time will come
No allies in the world can save you
From the punishment in Jahannam

GENOCIDE

The truth appears
Different to everyone
Although there is only one truth
In different ways it's spun

The spinning is done by people
Who only care for their own gain
Telling lies as truth
No matter if they cause pain

This is the reason
Some support a genocide
There's strong greed in their hearts
That's the truth upon which they abide

CRIMES

Someone help me contain my rage
      That wants to flow with every view
With every tear I see a mother shed
      Or the orphans whose blood you drew

Someone help me contain my emotions
      That wants to flow every time
When I clearly see an ethnic cleansing
      And a genocide that is deemed not a crime

SPINELESS

How many more massacres must happen
Until the people stop
Voting for criminal devils
Who currently are at the top

You think you are safe
From such a horrendous crime
If they can do that to babies
They'll do it to you at the drop of a dime

We are a means to an end
Worse, people without a spine
If we don't fight this genocide
That is happening now in PALESTINE

BREAKING OUR FAST

I cannot even fathom
What you are going through
I can eat again at night
Will you break your fast too?

Or will you be forced
To fast with no end in sight
Forced by people who claim
Your land is their birthright

How wonderful it would be
If I could share my food with you
Helping you in your hardship
And to gain Allah's mercy too

WIDE AWAKE

I AM WIDE AWAKE
But my hands are tied
I am drowning in despair
SO MANY INNOCENTS HAVE DIED

Before you ask, they haven't just died
BUT WERE RUTHLESSLY KILLED
By GODLESS people
Who won't admit their guilt

Their victim card long expired
Because I am not the only one AWAKE
THE WORLD SEES THEM FOR WHAT THEY ARE
Godless and fake

NEVER MEANT

You were never meant to be born
Shot in your mother's womb
For the sole crime of being Palestinian
Your five-year-old brother left orphaned in that room

There are no innocent people in Gaza
This is what the terrorists spew
This is how they justify genocide
And how they justify killing you

Your story is one of many
Because some hearts are made of stone
Thus, they keep committing unthinkable crimes
They will reap what they have sown

AFTER THE HORN IS BLOWN

The seventh of October
Is 18 days from now
Almost a year of killing past
And it continues, I don't know how

How can the world just watch
And provide the weapons for the crime
The children are the targets
Destroying a generation before their prime

Some were killed in their tents
At night while they slept
Others when getting bread
Lying later on the road dead

A next generation missing
The land grab plan in place
No more resistance with the occupation
Which is a human disgrace

I cannot fathom how
Anyone can stand behind this
Supporting the massacres of people
While enjoying worldly bliss

The people will be dragging
The oppressors to Allah's throne
And justice will be done
After the horn is blown

OLIVE TREES

There used to be a time
Where they lived carefree
Harvesting their olives
From 2000-year-old trees

There used to be a time
Where they did not ignore a plea
Inviting them to their land
When their own they had to flee

There used to be a time
Where they only owned the keys
For an ancestral home
Stolen by criminals with ease

There used to be a time
When they were the ones to flee
The colonial terrorists
Committing killing sprees

Now times have changed
We hope
From the river to the sea
PALESTINE WILL BE FREE

HIND RAJAB

She was only five years old
Caught in the colonial crossfire
Don't fight back her people were told
But an open-air prison is never an option

She was fleeing to a safe zone
No zone is safe in the strip
Her family in the car dead
Her pleas made the world skip

The world could not come to her aid
And the men who did died too
Her memory will never fade
Hind Rajab we will not forget you

Hind is one of many children
Who were killed for mere sport
For every killing justice will be served
In front of the Almighty's court

JUSTICE

Every time I think
It can't get any worse
In my mind I shrink
To horrors too perverse

A child without a head
Others in plastic bags
Shabaan burning alive in bed
Ignored were the white flags

Your lies a decoy
But the truth will come to light
Our tears a means of joy
Because they will get their right

FIRE'S HISS

Your Dunya cut short
Replaced by an akhira full of bliss
Your killers thought they won
Their akhira filled with fire's hiss

WHITE CLOTH

Cloth, white as snow
With a light red glow
The voices around grow

Despair, shock and pain
They ran to safety in vain
And still they were slain

We are all on time lent
To Allah we will be sent
And in Jannah we hopefully will end

WITNESS

I saw a burned body today
And my eyes looked away
For my heart it was too late
It stared and filled with hate
I know this feeling well
So, I won't stay and dwell
I already dispelled rage
To keep my heart uncaged

But the drones above them keep humming
So, the pictures keep on coming

THE GATEKEEPER

You are given more time
To dig a little deeper
To commit more crime
To meet the gatekeeper

He will not look nice
In front of the fires of hell
Your heart a block of ice
It will melt in its shell

You will never escape this place
The gatekeeper will make sure
Your punishment will know no grave
Which you will not be able to endure

ADVISOR

I   feel   hate
For your kind
Entitled   in   your   core
Hearts and eyes blind

You are resigned
To   steal   land
Kill   whoever   you   find
Claiming it was self-defense

You came here
Your plans outlined
To   eradicate   a   people
Who welcomed you blind

Your actions combined
And   lacking   humanity
Your   cruelty   quite   refined
Shaitan your closest advisor

RESISTANCE

EYES – shut tight
MIND – open wide
Soil in our palms
Stolen with a lie

Mind – NOW PLOTTING
Eyes – NOW DRIED
It was never yours to take
We will resist your apartheid!

LITTLE HANDS

The world is still silent
While babies are buried alive
Looking through tiny holes
Waiting for emergency to arrive

Its little hand stretched out
Seeking comfort from his fear
Recovery is a challenge
His survival – not clear

WARM

When you say it rains
Do you mean the drops of pain
Or the RAGE in my veins

For an evil done
To children with no guns
With no consequences – absolutely none

Supported by people in the west
Who claim decency in their chests
Pursuing their evil conquest

Some even stand on lookout towers
Viewing rubbles replace flowers
And killings that happen at all hours

So, no, rain would be the norm
These are times of a storm
Gushing dark red and warm

RED POPPIES

Red poppies absent for a while
But rubble pile upon pile upon pile

A field of stones
Blending in with their bones

Too many have gone home

Leaving this earth with a smile
Hoping not to stand trial
Their Jannah visible for miles

There they wait for the day of days
Where evil will end in the blaze
Their worldly gains forgotten in the haze

While we see rubble, they see poppies
But no worldly copy

The ones no eyes have seen yet

IRELAND

The prize goes to Ireland
With a people of moral stand
Not afraid to land a hand

They know how it feels
When oppressors steal meals
And starvation is on one's heals

They call it as it is

No exception for the crime
No underhanded dime

They even opened a museum

Instead of an embassy
Filled with ideology of supremacy
With evil tendency
More like devilry
With no credibility

Let the pictures speak for themselves

They claim not to hurt the innocent

But their claims are lies
Bodies piling up to the skies
While they fill the world with spies
You do not want those ties

So good riddance to them

Ireland will stand with pride
Against this genocide

ALIVE

Black, White Green
The land of Falestine

I heard the pin drop
And the following pop pop

No

It wasn't a pin
Have goose bumps on my skin

Eyes wide

Looking to the sky

No more people on the street
Ducking, running, swift and fleet

Black, White, Green, and Red
The child bled but is not dead

THE GUILT

The guilt of going to sleep
Warm, comfy
A steady heartbeat

It escapes, a comforting sigh
I don't see the sky
From my bed

The walls protect me from sound
My bed not a hard ground
Plenty of warmth to be found
The guilt of going to sleep

MAZE OF LIFE

My heart weeps
While my soul rejoices
Gone are their laughter
We will remember their voices
We will remember their choices

To be steadfast against tyranny
With bravery as their currency
Paying the ultimate price

This life is temporary anyways
Like going through a maze
Leading to the next phase
With more rays
And less haze

So, we rejoice in their struggle
And the immense rewards for their trouble
With the ultimate reward of Jannah

PERCEPTION

Perception is reality
Of the world I see around me

No need to convince you
Though the things I perceive are true

They are common sense
Understandable even to the most dense

Like the sky is blue
The tree because of the sun grew

In the mornings there is dew
And in spring the flowers grow anew

OR

Killing innocent children is an evil deed
Done by people with hearts of greed

While the world with leaders plead
They continue killing with unprecedented speed

Perception is reality
Of the evil you commit around me

You will answer for it at the end
And the fire will not be your friend

EID

Today is EID
What should be a joyous day
Instead of candies and presents
Among rubble they have to pray

Followed by a humble Eid meal
Of a little bit of bread
Some can even share it
Because their family is not yet dead

And still their praise of Allah never fails
Their strength, a beacon for us all
Holding tight to this precious land
Until the oppression falls

COWARDS

The world has seen plenty of cowards
Your Army is not the first
Your bravery determined by weapons
Your minds, quite disturbed

Only a fool believes he is strong
When the opponent is five years old
Congratulations coward
The five-year-old is the one who's bold

He has strength and courage
In the face of your full gear
Your presence a reminder
Who he will never grow to fear

You see, his reliance lies with Allah
Who's help is near
He will only feel pity for you
But never fear, never fear!

JOURNALIST

For every Journalist you kill
Ten will rise

To document their strength
And your crimes

You will never silence their voices
Or their choices, to stay in their land

To stand strong against an oppressor
      an aggressor
           and a possessor
                 of cowardice

your evil deeds
while you kill with ease
will continue to sow retaliatory seeds

Don't play the victim

When you choose to steal land
From people who gave you a hand
When you had nothing

DRIZZLE

We started off like a drizzle
Tiny drops barely noticeable first
Our voices needed more of something
They needed an outburst

This made the rain moderate
The drops became bigger now
Our voices were starting to be heard
Through gatherings they'd plough

So, we gained momentum
The heavy rain drops now steady and loud
We flood the cities and streets
Our voices strongly united and proud

The torrential rain is next
In the stages of rain
Our voices flash flooding
Unstoppable then, free rein

100 WORDS
SHORT STORIES

ANNE AND HIND

We all heard of the little Jewish girl that hid in the closet with her family.

Her name, Anne Frank.

She and her family were forced to live at night, stuck in the dark during the day due to fear of discovery.

Her childhood, until then a happy one.

We all heard the phone call of the little Muslim girl stuck in the car with her dead family.

Her name, Hind Rajab.

Injured and in extreme fear, she begged for help.

Anne was gassed; Hind was shot with over three hundred bullets.

Both killed by people with a racial ideology.

ON FIRE

It was fire, I knew that much, but what was on fire?

I didn't know at first what I was looking at.

      Was it a house, a bed, a human?

No, that couldn't be a human lying helpless in bed in a tent.

      But it was. It was a young man attached to an IV.

Now I saw it clear, his hand, his arm, his head.

      He was on fire, and I couldn't do a single thing to help him.

All I could do was watch it happen, because if I had looked away, I would have been guilty too.

ROOTS

He is not European enough as he enters his parents'
land.

His passport clearly shows he is, but his birth city,
Beirut, does not, his tan features do not, and his black
beard screams he is not.

He is definitely not European enough.

He grew up a refugee, now he visits his roots, the land
of his parents, grandparents, great grandparents. His
heritage but apparently not his land.

He is held in custody for not being European enough.

He is held for hours, interrogated, asking for
information he does not have. He is only visiting, not
reclaiming his stolen land.

NO ESCAPE

A toddler's limp body is held high by his screaming father, moments after clawing it out from under the rubble.

The glow emitting from his bombed home, a contrast to my dimmed lights.

His face, gray and shining with sweat, but I can clearly see anguish and desperation.

The adrenalin from the blast still pumping; now mixed with the shock of the aftermath, of holding his headless baby.

I realize too late he is holding only parts of his child.

My anguish could never match his, my anger could never match his.

I can turn off my phone, he cannot escape.

SONG

I heard you singing today, while you were walking towards gunfire.

It was a beautiful song, and if I had closed my eyes, I would have thought you were in the most beautiful location, and not in the midst of rubble.

I would have thought, judging from the melodious tune and the calmness of your voice, that you hadn't seen a bad day in a long time.

 I would have thought you were completely content.

But I didn't close my eyes, I couldn't close my eyes to the scene of a tank in the midst of Gaza shooting at civilians.

ON THE BROKEN STAIRCASE

On the broken staircase were helpers, first responders, civilians who came to the rescue. They tried to rescue what was left of a group of journalists who were blown up on the rooftop of the hospital.

The place most reliable for its internet. A hub for Journalists. A place news of the atrocities committed in Gaza spread from.

A place usually known for having a morgue in the basement, not the rooftop. The only thing that was spread on that day were pictures of dead journalists and their helpers on the broken staircase, because they told a story of oppression.

IF MY NAME WAS

If my name was Jason, Monica, or Benjamin I would be in the news. Stories would be written about me, how I am sleeping in a tent, how I can't go to school anymore, how my home was destroyed, how I am still at risk of getting hit by nightly bombings, and how I am starving to death.

I would be on the front page, on every news channel, and every social media platform.

But my name is not Jason, Monica, or Benjamin.

My name is Rayan. I am not on the news and will never make the front page.

STILL

They were lifting a massive rock from her lifeless body. She lay on her belly very still. One could mistakenly think she was taking a nap on a meadow.

But she wasn't.

Her fragile body lay on rubble covered in dust, dirt, and debris with blood on her face and body. She was still, oh so still.

I scrolled away, and then back, and then I scrolled away not being able to control my tears.

How could the world not come to her rescue?

How could we let her lie in rubble under a rock instead of a meadow?

How?

LOVE

He was lying on the comfy bed with the IV hanging from his tiny arm. His face as he looked at him, shone with the most beautiful smile. He was professing his admiration to a man who with his twenty-some years could have been his father. His soul was not mimicking his surroundings. His eyes were still full of life.

Next…

He was lying on a metal bed, cold, sterile with only a blanket. His IV was gone, his three-year-old arms tucked under the white blanket. His eyes and mouth half open. Gone was his smile, gone was his soul.

PRACTICAL

I heard you say, "I wish I had died."

How can a child, not older than ten, wish such a wish?

Easy!

Being dead would alleviate the pain of losing a mother,
father, siblings, uncles, aunts, cousins, grandparents,
friends. It would alleviate the fear of being struck,
maimed, or burned alive. It would alleviate the pain of
hunger caused by force starvation. It would alleviate the
struggle of constant displacement, of not having a bed
to sleep on, a roof above, a blanket for warmth.

Gaza's children have become practical.

Being dead would solve all their problems right now.

FOAM

The Hadith said, "Like the foam of the ocean." We will be many, but we will be weak and useless. Our distraction, the love for this Dunya.

As if we could take anything with us when we die.

As if it were more beautiful than Jannah.

As if it were going to make us happy.

As if it were worth more than a fly's wing.

Our deeds are the only thing we will take with us. It does not even come close to Jannah, it will never make us happy, **it is not even worth the wing of a fly.**

BAKING BREAD

The first time I saw you baking bread, you were highlighting the loss of your friend. You were challenging each other to see who could shape the dough, throw it in the air, lay it on the cushion, and put it on the dome-shaped oven the quickest.

Just two friends having fun in the midst of occupation and displacement, in the midst of bombing and destruction, in the midst of slaughter and forced mass starvation.

The small wooden countertop, covered in flour dust. Your smiling faces were also covered in flour dust; your background, however, was covered in demolition dust.

WINDOW

Another long shift was ongoing. I could imagine today felt as long as his entire life and then some.

Time didn't stop, the number of injured coming in didn't stop, so he and all the other nurses and doctors kept going.

No time for breaks, barely time for naps between his shifts, no possibility to get some fresh air, not even at the window.

He stood in the stuffy hallway of the half-destroyed hospital consulting a colleague when he collapsed with a gunshot wound to his head.

He was standing too close to the window, exactly a room's length away.

FAILED

They were kidnapped. They were tortured. They were mutilated. They were killed.

They were kidnapped. They were tortured. They were mutilated. They were killed.

They were kidnapped. They were tortured. They were mutilated. They were killed.

I said it over and over and over again. No matter how many times I said it, it did not change the fact that the world let them be kidnapped, be tortured, be mutilated, and be killed. The world was fine with their bodies being returned in bags with numbers on them.

The world has failed these kidnapped, tortured, mutilated, killed individuals. Just failed.

TO DO LIST

I wake up from a fitful sleep. The loud explosions, the cold, and the bugs crawling on my family have kept me awake most of the night.

I make a mental note of my *"to-do"* list for today. Even if I owned a pen and paper, I would not have to write this down. It is redundant. It has been etched into my brain for a while. I think I will be able to recount it to my grandchildren if I survive this.

- *Find food*
- *Find blankets*
- *Find a tent*
- *Find a safe location*
- *Find wood*
- *Find pen and paper*

ABOUT THE AUTHOR

C. Tarantino is a writer based between continents. Her work is inspired by joyous moments, grief, transformation, and life experiences. She holds a bachelor's degree in English Literature and brings her love of language and reflection into every piece she writes.

When she isn't writing, she embraces her "scanner" nature — exploring many interests and creative outlets.